This book belongs to

Jena H Monks

Jena Hannh Monks

BBC
CHILDREN'S BOOKS
Published by the Penguin Group
Penguin Books Ltd, 80 Strand, London WC2R 0RL, England
Penguin Group (USA) Inc., 375 Hudson Street, New York, New York 10014, USA
Penguin Group (Australia) Ltd, 250 Camberwell Road, Camberwell, Victoria 3124, Australia
(a division of Pearson Australia Group Pty Ltd)
Canada, India, New Zealand, South Africa
First published by BBC Children's Books, 2006
This edition produced for The Book People Ltd, Hall Wood Avenue,
Haydock, St Helens, WA11 9UL
10 9 8 7 6 5 4 3 2 1

Photography by Steve Shott. With additional recipes by Fiona Munro.

ISBN 13: 978-1-40590-342-4
Printed in China

TED SMART

Contents

Before You Start Cooking

1 Always wash your hands before you start cooking, and after handling any raw food.

2 Check you have all the ingredients and utensils that you need to make the recipe.

3 Measure and prepare any ingredients you need, before you start to cook. Weigh the ingredients in either grams or ounces, but don't mix the measurements up.

4 Always ask your grown-up helper to help you with chopping or measuring, and to move things in and out of the oven or freezer for you. Be sure that food is cooked all the way through.

5 Be careful not to touch anything that has just come out of the oven – it will be HOT HOT HOT! Always leave the food to cool down.

Healthy Hints for Grown-up Helpers

1 You can look at using low fat alternatives for recipes that include cheese, cream, butter or yogurt.

2 Try experimenting with lower quantities of sugar, honey and jam for healthier teeth.

3 Food colouring can cause hyperactivity in children and its use is only optional in these recipes.

4 Always ensure children wash their hands before and during cooking.

5 When trying new foods for the first time, be aware that some may cause allergic reactions.

Look out for these symbols:

grown-up to help

no cooking involved

Vegetable House

Ingredients – makes one house

- 375g/13oz ready-made, defrosted puff pastry
- a sprinkle of flour
- 100g/$3\frac{1}{2}$oz canned lentils
- 1 teaspoon mild curry powder
- mixed vegetables
- 1 egg
- 1 tablespoon milk

1 Ask your grown-up helper to preheat the oven to 220C/425F/gas mark 7. Line a baking tray with greaseproof paper.

2 Sprinkle some flour on a clean work surface and roll out the puff pastry. Ask your grown-up helper to cut out the shape of a house. Prick some holes in it with a fork, and place it on the baking tray.

3 Crack the egg on to a saucer. Place a small pastry cutter over the yolk, and carefully pour the white away, into a small bowl. Put the yolk into a separate bowl. (Wash your hands after handling the raw egg.) Whisk the yolk with a fork, to make 'glue' for the house.

4 Cut some strips of pastry to go around the edges of the house, and use a pastry brush and the egg yolk to stick them in place. Use the rest of the yolk to paint over the whole house.

5 Ask your grown-up helper to put it in the oven for about ten minutes, or until the pastry is golden.

6 Ask your grown-up helper to cut the mixed vegetables into the shapes you need to decorate your house. You could use tomato pieces as roof tiles, broccoli for a little tree, or carrot cubes for bricks. Ask your grown-up helper to steam or boil the vegetables for a couple of minutes, until they are tender.

7 At the same time, drain the lentils and put them in a pan with the curry powder and two tablespoons of water. Ask your grown-up helper to heat them up.

8 Ask your grown-up helper to remove the house from the oven and put it on a plate. Spoon the lentil mixture into the house, and decorate it with your mixed vegetables.

9 Serve while hot.

Tortoise Salad

Ingredients
- 5 tablespoons apple juice
- juice of 1 lemon
- 2 tablespoons olive oil
- 1 pitta bread
- 2 tablespoons soft cheese
- 2 cherry tomatoes, sliced in half
- 1 apple, sliced
- a few lettuce leaves
- 2 raisins

1 Ask your grown-up helper to toast the pitta bread and leave it to cool. Cut it in half to form two pockets.

2 One half will be the tortoise's shell. Spread some soft cheese inside it and stuff it with lettuce and slices of apple. Stand it up on the plate.

3 Ask your grown-up helper to cut a small piece off the other half of the pitta bread, then fill it with soft cheese and lettuce to make the tortoise's head. Use some of the cheese to stick the raisins on as eyes.

4 Ask your grown-up helper to cut the remaining piece of pitta into four pieces and place these around the tortoise as legs.

5 Use half a cherry tomato for each foot. Arrange the rest of the salad around the tortoise.

6 To make the salad dressing, pour the apple juice, lemon juice and olive oil into a jar. Screw on the lid and shake it up to mix the ingredients.

7 Pour the dressing over the salad, and serve.

Herby Paint Pots

Ingredients

Green dip
- I cup Greek yogurt
- ½ cup grated cucumber
- a few sprigs mint, finely chopped
- I spring onion, finely chopped

Pink dip
- I cup Greek yogurt
- I pre-cooked, grated beetroot
- I spring onion, finely chopped
- a tablespoon of chives, finely chopped

You will also need:
- 2 sticks celery, two empty yogurt pots, pink and green card, round-ended scissors and some sticky tape.

I To make the green dip, place a cup of Greek yogurt into a mixing bowl. Add the grated cucumber, spring onion and mint, and stir.

2 Using a different mixing bowl, make the pink dip by mixing a cup of Greek yogurt with the grated beetroot, spring onion and chopped chives.

3 Put both bowls in the fridge to chill while you make your paint pots and brushes.

4 Cut the pink and green card into strips and stick them around the yogurt pots. Fill them with the dips using a teaspoon.

5 Ask your grown-up helper to help you make the brushes by splitting the celery down the middle so that you have long, thin sticks. Carefully snip the ends to look like bristles.

You could also use carrots, asparagus or breadsticks for your paintbrushes.

Elfy Mushrooms

Ingredients
- packet mushrooms
- ½ cup soft cheese
- 2 slices bread
- ½ onion, finely chopped
- 1 egg
- 4 slices cheese
- packet radishes

1 Ask your grown-up helper to preheat the oven to 180C/350F/gas mark 4.

2 Wash the mushrooms and take out the stalks.

3 Ask your grown-up helper to chop up the stalks and mix with the onion in a bowl.

4 Crumble up the slices of bread with your fingers, until they are breadcrumbs. Add this to the bowl, with a pinch of salt and pepper.

5 Add in most of the soft cheese and the egg. Stir well.

6 Put a teaspoon of the mixture into each mushroom. Place them on a greased baking tray.

7 Cut the slices of cheese into small squares and put a square of cheese onto the top of each filled mushroom. Ask your grown-up helper to put them in the oven for fifteen minutes.

8 Ask your grown-up helper to chop the heads and tails off the radishes. Use a little soft cheese to stick the radishes to the mushrooms as stalks.

Postman's Parcels

Ingredients
- ready-made pancakes
- 250g/9oz ricotta cheese
- ½ cup frozen spinach
- 2 tomatoes, chopped up
- ½ onion, finely chopped
- 2 tablespoons of olive oil
- ¼ cucumber, sliced
- 1 olive, sliced
- small squares of cheese

1 Ask your grown-up helper to heat the oil in a pan and cook the onion until soft. Stir in the tomatoes and the spinach and cook for another five minutes.

2 Add the ricotta cheese and put the mixture to one side.

3 Ask your grown-up helper to heat up each pancake and turn it out onto a plate. Spoon two heaped tablespoons of the spinach mixture into the middle of each pancake.

4 Fold up the bottom part, and then fold in the sides. Finally, fold over the top to make it look like an envelope.

5 Carefully flip the envelope over, so that the front is at the top.

Beany Giant

Ingredients
- 1 egg
- 3 sausages
- 1 large baking potato
- 1 small can baked beans

1 Ask your grown-up helper to place the potato on a baking tray and bake for about forty minutes at 230C/450F/ gas mark 8.

2 Ask your grown-up helper to boil the egg for ten minutes and then rinse under a cold tap.

3 Ask your grown-up helper to grill the three sausages slowly, making sure they are cooked all the way through and to heat the beans up in a saucepan.

4 Ask your grown-up helper to take the potato out of the oven and cut in half on a plate. This will be the giant's eyes.

5 Roll the cold boiled egg between your hand and the work surface, to crack the shell. Peel the egg and cut two slices from it, to finish the eyes.

6 Cut two of the sausages in half and place two halves above the eyes for eyebrows and the other two as a mouth. Use the third as a nose.

7 Spoon the beans over the top as hair and at the bottom for a beard.

Veggie Sandcastles

Ingredients
- 1 onion, finely chopped
- 1 teaspoon turmeric
- 1 cup long grain rice
- ½ cup frozen peas
- 5 large tomatoes, chopped
- ½ red pepper, deseeded and finely chopped
- 2 cups water
- olive oil

If you like, you can make a flag, and pop it in the top of your castle.

1 Ask your grown-up helper to heat some olive oil in a saucepan. Add the onion, peppers and turmeric and cook for five minutes.

2 Ask your grown-up helper to add the rice and stir. Pour in the chopped tomatoes and two cups of water. Bring to the boil and then simmer for fifteen minutes until the rice is soft. If the rice is looking dry, add a little extra water.

3 Add the peas and cook for another five minutes, stirring gently. Take the pan off the heat.

4 Grease a plastic beaker with butter or margarine. This will be your sandcastle mould. Carefully fill it up with the rice mixture, and press down firmly with the back of a spoon. Leave it to cool for a couple of minutes.

5 Tip the mould upside down on a plate and gently remove your sandcastle.

Mermaid Soup

Ingredients
- 2 cups water
- I cube powdered vegetable stock
- I bunch Chinese rice noodles
- I cup shredded spinach
- I slice bread

I Ask your grown-up helper to boil the water in a pan and crumble in the stock cube. Stir until the stock has dissolved.

2 Break the noodles in half and add to the pan. Turn off the heat.

3 Toast the slice of bread.

4 Let the noodles soak for two minutes, then add the spinach and stir. Leave it for another two minutes to finish cooking.

5 When the toast is ready, use a fish-shaped cutter to cut out a fish shape or ask your grown-up helper to carefully cut you a fish shape.

6 Pour the soup into a bowl and top with the toasted fish to serve.

Croissant Dragon

Ingredients
- 1 olive
- 3 croissants
- 3 slices ham
- 1 cup grated cheese
- 1 black olive, or a raisin
- ½ red pepper, deseeded and sliced

1 Ask your grown-up helper to preheat the oven to 220C/425F/gas mark 7.

2 Ask your grown-up helper to slice all three croissants open lengthways.

3 Place a slice of ham and some grated cheese inside each croissant to make sandwiches. Cut one of the croissants in half.

4 Arrange the pieces of croissant on a greased baking tray. Place two croissants down for the body and the tail. Use the two halves of croissant to make a head and a wing.

5 Sprinkle the remaining grated cheese all over the dragon and ask your grown-up helper to place it in the oven. Take the dragon out when the cheese has melted. This will take about eight to ten minutes. Keep an eye on it to make sure the cheese doesn't burn.

6 When the dragon has cooled enough to handle, place it on a large plate.

7 Use half an olive, or a raisin, as the dragon's eye.

8 Use the slices of red pepper to make flames coming out of the dragon's mouth, and four short slices as the dragon's feet.

Fab Footballs

Ingredients
- tray of cress
- 2 large potatoes, chopped
- $\frac{1}{2}$ cup sesame seeds
- $\frac{1}{2}$ cup cheese, grated
- 1 egg
- 6 black olives, chopped into little pieces

You will also need:
- three ice lolly sticks, sticky tape and netting from a bag of oranges to make your goal
- a slice of toast

1 Ask your grown-up helper to preheat the oven to 230C/450F/gas mark 8.

2 Place the potatoes in a pan and cover with cold water. Ask your grown-up helper to boil the potatoes until they are soft. Drain the water from the potatoes and place them in a bowl. Mash them up until smooth with a potato masher.

3 Add the egg, the cheese and half of the cress. Use a fork to mix it all together.

4 Sprinkle some sesame seeds onto a plate. With clean hands, roll the potato mixture into small balls, then roll these in the sesame seeds to coat them. Place them on a greased baking tray.

5 Carefully push little pieces of olive onto each one, to make them look like small footballs.

6 Ask your grown-up helper to bake them on the top shelf of the oven, for about ten minutes.

7 Tape the lolly sticks together in a bridge shape, and use the orange netting bag to make a net for your goal. Stand the goal in the slice of toast, and decorate with the cress and footballs to serve.

Please be aware that sesame seeds can cause an allergic reaction, similar to peanuts, and should be used with caution.

Humpty Salad

Ingredients
- 2 eggs
- a few lettuce leaves
- 5 slices cucumber
- 1 spring onion, finely chopped
- 2 tablespoons mayonnaise
- $\frac{1}{2}$ lemon
- salt and pepper
- red and blue food colouring, optional

1. Ask your grown-up helper to boil the eggs for ten minutes.
2. Carefully remove the eggs from the pan, and run them under cold water until they have cooled down.
3. Half fill two glasses with cold water and mix a teaspoon of blue food colouring in one, and red in the other.
4. Carefully tap the eggs all over to crack the shell, but don't remove it yet.
5. Place one egg in each of the glasses of coloured water. Leave them in the fridge over night.
6. Remove the eggshells and cut the eggs in half lengthways, and then in half again.
7. Place each of the egg pieces in a lettuce leaf and arrange on a plate. Add the five cucumber slices in a flower pattern on the top.
8. Squeeze half a lemon with a lemon squeezer. Mix the juice with two tablespoons of mayonnaise and some salt and pepper. Pour this into the centre of the cucumber flower and sprinkle with spring onion to serve.

You will need to start this recipe the day before you want to eat it, if you want to colour the eggs. You can leave the eggs white if you want to eat the salad straight away.

Neenaw Sirens

Ingredients

- $\frac{1}{2}$ onion, chopped
- $\frac{1}{2}$ cup tofu, chopped
- $\frac{1}{2}$ cup couscous
- 1 cup water
- 2 tablespoons olive oil
- 1 red pepper, deseeded and finely diced
- 2 red peppers, tops cut off and deseeded, to fill

1 Ask your grown-up helper to preheat the oven to 200C/390F/gas mark 6.

2 Ask your grown-up helper to add the chopped onion and pepper to a saucepan with two tablespoons of olive oil.

3 Stir and cook the mixture until it is soft, and then add the tofu. Stir and cook for a couple more minutes.

4 Add the couscous and the water to the mixture and bring to the boil. Turn down to simmer for two minutes, then cover and turn off the heat. Leave for five minutes, or until the water has all gone.

5 Spoon the cooked mixture into the peppers. Pack the mixture down tightly, pressing down with a spoon.

6 Pop the peppers onto a greased baking tray and ask a grown-up helper to put them in the oven for thirty minutes, until cooked.

Hot Rod Racer

Ingredients
- sausage
- finger roll
- squeezy tomato sauce
- 4 thick slices cucumber

You will also need:
- some card, coloured pens or pencils, an ice lolly stick, round-ended scissors and some sticky tape.

1 Ask your grown-up helper to cut a slit down the middle of the finger roll, and to fry or grill the sausage for you, until it is cooked all the way through.

2 Draw your racing driver on a piece of card. Cut him or her out and stick an ice lolly stick on the back with sticky tape.

3 When the sausage is cooked, put it in the bun and position the cucumber slices at the sides as wheels.

4 Squirt ketchup in a wavy pattern along the top of your sausage.

5 Stick the driver in the hot rod racer to serve.

Pizza Shield

Ingredients

- 200g/$7\frac{1}{2}$oz self-raising flour
- 50g/2oz butter or margarine
- 1 cup grated cheese
- 4 tablespoons milk
- 1 tin chopped tomatoes
- $\frac{1}{4}$ pepper, deseeded and sliced
- 2 mushrooms, cleaned and sliced
- $\frac{1}{2}$ small onion, chopped

1 Ask your grown-up helper to preheat the oven to 220C/425F/gas mark 7.

2 Put the flour into a bowl and rub the butter or margarine into the flour with your hands, until it looks like breadcrumbs.

3 Stir the milk into the mixture. Use a spoon at first, and then use your hands to knead the mixture into a firm dough.

4 Sprinkle a little bit of flour onto a clean surface and roll the dough out flat with a rolling pin.

5 Ask your grown-up helper to cut the dough into a shield shape, and place it on a greased baking tray.

6 Use the spare dough to make two thin sausages and lay these in a cross shape over the shield, to divide it into four sections.

7 Spread the tomatoes evenly over the pizza base. Then sprinkle the cheese all over it. Put your remaining ingredients in each section.

8 Ask your grown-up helper to place the pizza in the oven for fifteen to twenty minutes until the dough has baked, and the cheese is melted and golden.

Flowery Basket Sandwiches

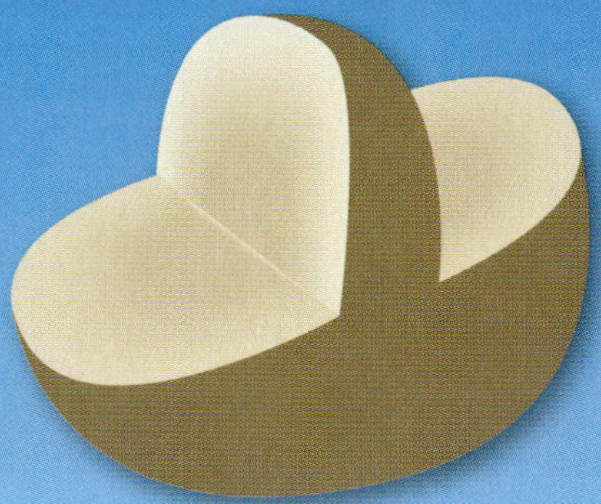

Ingredients – 1 sandwich
- 1 wholemeal bread roll
- 2 cherry tomatoes
- 2 radishes
- 2 slices cheddar cheese
- a bunch of parsley
- 4 pineapple chunks

You will also need:
- a flower-shaped cutter
- short, thin straws

1 Ask your grown-up helper to cut the bread roll into the basket shape shown in the diagram.

2 Pull out the bread from underneath the 'handle' to hollow out the basket.

3 Use a cutter to cut flower shapes out of the cheese slices. If you don't have a flower-shaped cutter, ask your grown-up helper to cut some cheese shapes out for you with a knife.

4 Poke the flowers onto the straws and top each one with a piece of pineapple. Put the flowers into the basket.

5 Stick the tomatoes and radishes on different straws, and place these in the basket, too.

6 Arrange the parsley around the basket to make leaves for the flowers.

Duck Dippers

Ingredients - makes about 12 dippers
- 20 cream crackers
- 1 cup cheddar cheese, finely grated
- 1 large tablespoon butter or margarine
- 2 eggs
- raisins
- $\frac{1}{2}$ cup cream cheese
- $\frac{1}{2}$ cup pineapple chunks
- a little flour

You will also need:
- a duck-shaped cutter

1 Ask your grown-up helper to preheat the oven to 200C/400F/gas mark 6.

2 Put the crackers in a plastic bowl and crush them into very fine crumbs, with the end of a rolling pin.

3 With clean hands, rub the butter or margarine into the crumbs. Make sure they are all coated.

4 Add the grated cheese and mix well. Then carefully crack the two eggs into the mixture, and stir with a fork.

5 As it gets firmer, use your hands to mix it into a dough.

6 Sprinkle some flour onto a clean work surface, and roll the dough out flat.

7 Cut out some ducks with your cutter or ask your grown-up helper to cut some duck shapes for you with a knife and place them on a lightly greased baking tray.

8 Place a raisin on each one for an eye.

9 Ask your grown-up helper to bake them in the oven for 10-15 minutes.

10 While they are cooking, mix the pineapple chunks and the cream cheese in a bowl, to make your dip. Allow the dippers to cool and place them around your dip pond to serve.

Cheesy Mice

Ingredients – makes 5 mice

- I packet soft cheese
- 2 radishes, sliced into small circles
- I radish, cut into triangles
- raisins
- a bunch of chives
- 10 small cheese crackers
- I apple, sliced
- slices of cheddar cheese

1 Take a cracker and cover it with a slice of cheese and a slice of apple. Place another cracker on top to make a sandwich.

2 Divide the soft cheese into five portions and roll each one into an egg shape.

3 Place an egg-shaped ball of cheese on top of each sandwich.

4 Take two circles of radish and place them on the cheese as ears.

5 Use a small triangle of radish as a nose and raisins for eyes.

6 Use chives to make a tail and whiskers for your little mouse.

Traffic Light Pinwheel Sandwiches

Ingredients – makes about 50 tiny sandwiches

- 6 slices wholemeal bread
- 6 tablespoons cream cheese
- 2 tablespoons mayonnaise
- ½ green pepper, sliced
- ½ yellow pepper, sliced
- ½ red pepper, sliced

1 Mix the cream cheese with the mayonnaise in a bowl.

2 Cut the crusts off the bread and lightly roll out each slice with a rolling pin. Spread each slice with the cream cheese mixture.

3 Put pieces of pepper across the end of each slice of bread. Make two slices of bread with green pepper, two with yellow and two with red.

4 Roll the slices of bread up tightly around the pepper, and wrap each roll in cling film and store in the fridge.

5 When you are ready to serve the sandwiches, take them out of the fridge and slice them into circles.

Witches' Cauldrons

Ingredients – makes 6 cauldrons

- 6 small round potatoes
- 3 tablespoons grated cheddar cheese
- 2 tablespoons chives, finely chopped
- 2 tablespoons tinned sweetcorn
- 2 slices ham, cut into small pieces
- 6 long thin slices sweet pepper (any colour)

1 Ask your grown-up helper to preheat the oven to 200C/400F/gas mark 6.

2 Put the potatoes onto a lightly greased baking tray. If they roll about, cut a small piece from the base so they sit firmly.

3 Bake in the oven for about an hour. They are ready when you can easily slide a sharp knife into them. Ask your grown-up helper to do this for you.

4 When they are cool enough to handle, ask your grown-up helper to cut a circle about the size of a large coin from the top.

5 With a teaspoon, carefully scoop the potato out of the skin and into a small mixing bowl. Be careful not to break the skin if you can help it.

6 Add your grated cheese, chives, sweetcorn and ham to the potato and stir well. Scoop the mixture back into the skins.

7 Put your potatoes into a suitable heat-proof container and ask your grown-up helper to place them under a hot grill for about ten minutes, or until the filling is bubbling and turning brown. Don't worry if it starts to spill over the edge. This will make your cauldrons look more witchy!

8 Ask your grown-up helper to remove them from the grill and leave for a few minutes to cool down.

9 Take your strips of pepper and sink the ends of each strip into the sides of the potatoes to make a handle for your cauldron.

Deeply Dippy

Ingredients – makes enough for 6 people

- 3 red peppers, with stalks cut off
- 6 tablespoons cottage cheese
- 3 tablespoons natural yogurt
- 3 tablespoons runny honey
- $\frac{1}{2}$ a cucumber, cut into sticks
- 3 carrots, cut into sticks
- 1 green or yellow pepper, cut into sticks

1 Cut each pepper in half, across the middle.

2 Carefully scoop out the seeds with a teaspoon.

3 In a small bowl, mix the cottage cheese with the yogurt and honey.

4 Spoon the mixture into each pepper half.

5 Now fill each pepper with your colourful vegetable dippers!

Cheesy Feet

Ingredients - makes 3 feet

- 1 egg
- 250g/8oz ready-made puff pastry
- 100g/3oz ricotta or crumbled feta cheese
- 1 tablespoon tomato puree
- handful of torn basil leaves
- a little plain flour

You will also need:

- the foot template below

1 Ask your grown-up helper to preheat the oven to 220C/425F/gas mark 7.

2 Grease a baking sheet with a little butter or margarine.

3 Beat the egg in a jug with a fork.

4 Sprinkle the flour onto a clean work surface and use a rolling pin to roll the pastry into a large rectangle.

5 Brush the pastry with the beaten egg.

6 Using the back of a teaspoon, spread the tomato puree over one half of the pastry.

7 Spread the cheese over the tomato puree and sprinkle with the torn basil. Fold the other side of the pastry over it and press down gently.

8 Roll gently a couple more times until flat and the edges are sealed together.

9 Brush the surface of the pastry with egg and cut into three equal strips.

10 Using a blunt table knife, cut simple foot shapes into each strip, using the template opposite.

11 Use a fish slice to carefully put your feet on the greased baking sheet and ask your grown-up helper to put them in the oven for you.

12 Your cheesy feet will take about 15 minutes to cook. When they are ready they will be golden brown and puffy!

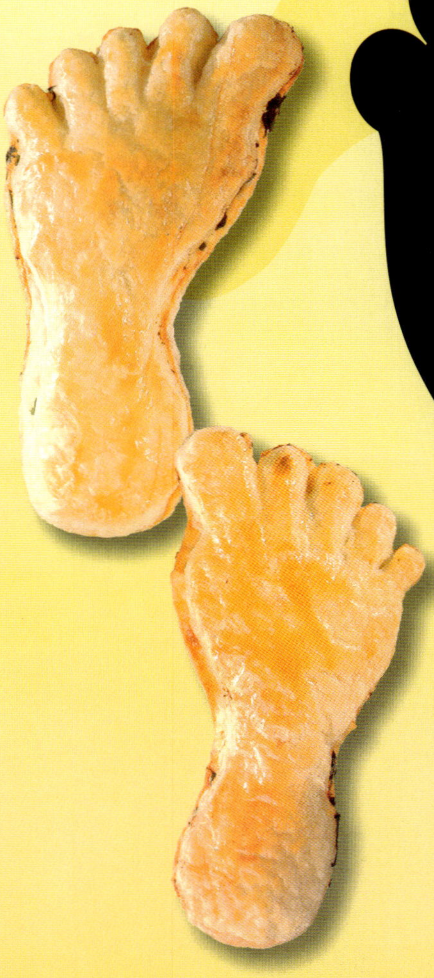

Froggy Feast

Ingredients – makes four frogs

- 4 green peppers, halved and deseeded
- 2 carrots, one sliced and one grated
- $\frac{1}{2}$ onion, finely chopped
- 100g/3$\frac{1}{2}$ oz couscous
- 200ml/7fl.oz water
- 1 vegetable stock cube
- sliced olives
- 25g/1oz cheddar, or other hard cheese
- 2 tablespoons olive oil, butter, or margarine

1 Ask your grown-up helper to preheat the oven to 230C/450F/gas mark 8.

2 Ask your grown-up helper to fry the onion and carrot for two minutes.

3 Add the water and stock cube and bring to the boil, then pour in the couscous. Stir well. Put a lid on the pan and take it off the heat.

4 Leave the mixture for about 5 minutes, then stir in a tablespoon of olive oil, butter or margarine.

5 Fill four of the pepper halves with couscous and wrap them in aluminium foil. Ask your grown-up helper to put them on a baking tray and place them in the oven for fifteen minutes.

6 Ask your grown-up helper to cut the remaining pepper halves into quarters, then cut them into feet shapes.

7 Place each cooked pepper on a plate and allow to cool. Arrange the pepper feet around them.

8 Use circles of cheese and slices of olive to make the frog's eyes, and slices of carrot for the frog's spots.

Gardener's Pickle

Ingredients – makes one jar

- 1 medium onion, peeled and sliced
- 2 red peppers, deseeded and sliced
- 2 yellow peppers, deseeded and sliced
- 1 heaped tablespoon salt
- 300ml/10fl oz distilled malt vinegar
- 1 teaspoon turmeric
- 1 teaspoon mustard seeds
- 150g/5oz granulated sugar

You will also need:

- a large, clean, sterilized jar with a lid
- paper and pencils
- sticky tape or glue
- circle of cloth
- elastic band or ribbon

1 Place all the sliced vegetables in a bowl with the salt, and mix well. Cover the bowl with cling film and leave it overnight.

2 Make a label with your paper and pens, and stick it to the front of the jar.

3 Rinse the vegetables with cold water to wash off the salt. Dry them with kitchen paper or a clean tea towel.

4 Put the vinegar in a saucepan with the mustard seeds, sugar and turmeric. Ask your grown-up helper to bring the mixture to the boil, then simmer for about ten minutes.

5 Ask your grown-up helper to add the vegetables and bring the mixture back to the boil. Cook for a couple of minutes and then remove from the heat.

6 Allow the mixture to cool, then spoon into the jar.

7 Screw the lid on tight and place the circle of cloth over the top. Put an elastic band or some ribbon around the lid of the jar, to hold it in place.

Jolly Jelly Boats

Ingredients
- half packet of jelly
- 250ml hot water
- 1 orange

You will also need:
- 2 straws
- coloured paper
- round-ended scissors
- sticky tape
- a pen or pencil

1 Ask your grown-up helper to cut the orange in half, and squeeze out the juice and the flesh. Keep the orange halves.

2 Ask your grown-up helper to mix the jelly with 250ml of warm water from the kettle, and dissolve all the jelly cubes by whisking them with a fork.

3 Balance the orange halves in cups so that they don't fall over and pour the jelly into them. Place the halves in the fridge for a few hours, until the jelly is set and wobbly.

4 Ask your grown-up helper to cut the jelly oranges in half again, to make four boats.

5 Cut a triangle out of the coloured card and write your name on it. Cut a piece of straw, and stick it to the card. Stick your jelly sail into your boat.

Monkey Baskets

Ingredients
- 2 large oranges
- 1 small apple, chopped
- 1 banana, peeled and sliced
- a few grapes
- juice of 1 lemon
- ½ cup desiccated coconut

1 Ask your grown-up helper to cut the tops off the oranges and use a knife to loosen all the flesh inside. Use a spoon to pull out the insides, then chop up the flesh into bite-sized pieces and put them into a bowl.

2 Add the chopped apple and grapes to the bowl.

3 Finally, add the sliced banana and lemon juice to the mixture.

4 Ask your grown-up helper to cut a zigzag pattern around the tops of the oranges with a pair of scissors.

5 Fill the hollowed out oranges with the fruit salad mixture, and sprinkle with desiccated coconut.

Mince Pie Moles

Ingredients - makes about 12

- 225g/8oz flour, half wholemeal, half white
- 100g/4oz butter or margarine, cut into pieces
- 3 tablespoons cold water
- 6 tablespoons mincemeat
- 25g/1oz raisins

1 Sift the flour into a bowl and add the butter or margarine. Rub it into the flour with your fingertips, until the mixture looks like breadcrumbs.

2 Add the cold water a little at a time, and stir with a wooden spoon. Once the mixture starts to stick together, knead it to make dough. Wrap the dough in cling film and place in the fridge for half an hour.

3 Lightly grease a bun tin and ask your grown-up helper to preheat the oven to 200C/400F/gas mark 6.

4 Sprinkle a little flour onto a clean work surface. Roll out the pastry with a rolling pin. Use your circle-shaped cutter to cut out some circles and place them in the bun tin.

5 Put a rounded teaspoon of mincemeat into each pastry case.

6 Use a blunt table knife to cut out two 'feet' for each mole. Cut semi-circles of pastry and shape them into cones for the moles' noses. Use little blobs of pastry for the eyes. Top the noses with raisins.

7 Ask your grown-up helper to place them in the oven for approximately fifteen minutes. Allow them to cool before eating.

Yeti Pear Pudding

Ingredients
- 50g/2oz pudding or short grain rice
- 600ml/21 fl. oz semi-skimmed milk
- 25g/1oz sugar
- a little butter or margarine
- 2 tablespoons jam, any flavour
- 2 pears, peeled, halved and cored

1 Lightly grease a baking dish and preheat the oven to 170C/300F/gas mark 3.

2 Put the rice, milk and sugar into the dish. Cover it with foil and ask your grown-up helper to place it on a baking tray in the oven, for approximately two hours, or until the mixture has thickened. Ask your grown-up helper to stir it a couple of times during the first hour, and remove it from the oven once it is ready.

3 Ask your grown-up helper to melt the jam in a pan until it is runny. Use a teaspoon to drip the jam over the rice pudding, to make snowflakes.

4 Use a blunt table knife to cut zig-zags around the top and bottom of the pear halves. Place them on top of the rice pudding and add raisins to make arms, legs and eyes for your yetis.

Flutterby Cakes

Ingredients

- 100g/$3\frac{1}{2}$ oz soft butter or margarine
- 100g/$3\frac{1}{2}$ oz caster sugar
- 100g/$3\frac{1}{2}$ oz self-raising flour
- 2 eggs
- jam, any flavour
- jelly sweets or icing pens (optional)
- paper cake cases

1 Ask your grown-up helper to preheat the oven to 180C/350F/gas mark 4.

2 Mix the butter or margarine and sugar together until creamy with either a wooden spoon or an electric whisk.

3 Crack two eggs into the mixture and beat them in.

4 Hold a sieve over the mixture and pour the flour into it. Gently shake the sieve from side to side, so that the flour falls through the holes and into the mixture. This makes the mixture less lumpy and will make your cakes light and fluffy.

5 Stir the flour into the mixture until it is fairly stiff.

6 Use a teaspoon to dollop the mixture into cake cases. There should be enough for about ten little cakes.

7 Ask your grown-up helper to pop them on a baking tray and place them in the oven for about fifteen minutes. Keep an eye on them to make sure they don't burn. When they are ready, leave them to cool down.

8 Ask your grown-up helper to carefully cut the top off each cake, so that you have a lid.

9 Spread jam onto the bottom half of each cake. Cut the lids in half and, if you like, decorate them with icing pens or jelly sweets. Arrange these on the top of each cake as butterfly wings.

Carrot Cakes

Ingredients

- 100g/3½ oz brown sugar
- 2 eggs
- 1 tablespoon sunflower oil
- 100g/3½ oz of self-raising flour
- 2 medium carrots, grated
- 1 cup raisins
- 1 tablespoon icing sugar
- 2 tablespoons cream cheese
- paper cake cases
- orange and green marzipan (optional)

1. Ask your grown-up helper to preheat the oven to 220C/420F/gas mark 7.
2. Put the sugar, eggs and oil into a big bowl. Use an electric whisk or a wooden spoon to mix it until creamy.
3. Fold in the flour.
4. Add the grated carrot and the raisins, and mix with a wooden spoon.
5. Use a teaspoon to fill up your paper cases, and place them on a baking tray. Ask your grown-up helper to put them in the oven for about twenty minutes.
6. Meanwhile, mix the cream cheese with the icing sugar and put it in the fridge for later.
7. If you are using marzipan, make some carrot-shaped decorations.
8. Ask your grown-up helper to remove the cakes from the oven and leave them to cool.
9. Use a spoon to spread the cream cheese icing on top of the cakes, and decorate each with a marzipan carrot.

Crispy Bricks

Ingredients
- 1 cup mini marshmallows
- 2 cups puffed rice cereal
- 2 tablespoons sugar
- 1 tablespoon cocoa
- 2 teaspoons water
- 2 tablespoons butter or margarine
- ice cube trays

1 Ask your grown-up helper to melt one tablespoon of butter over a low heat, and add the marshmallows.

2 Add the puffed rice and stir all the ingredients together.

3 Use a teaspoon to pack the mixture into ice cube trays. Leave the bricks to go cold, then put them in the fridge so that they set hard.

4 To make the icing, mix the remaining tablespoon of butter or margarine and the sugar, until you have a creamy mixture. Add the cocoa powder and the water to make a smooth paste.

5 When the bricks have set, ask your grown-up helper to help you remove them from the ice cube trays.

6 Use the chocolate icing mixture as cement to stick your bricks together.

Berry Ballerina

Ingredients
- 2 eggs
- 100g/3 ½ oz caster sugar
- ½ cup Greek yogurt
- 1 cup mixed berries
- greaseproof paper

You will also need:
- some card, colouring pens or pencils, sticky tape, round-ended scissors and a lolly stick.

1 Ask your grown-up helper to preheat the oven to 130C/250F/gas mark 0.5.

2 Crack the eggs and ask your grown-up helper to separate the yolks and whites into different bowls. Put the yolks to one side.

3 Whisk the egg whites until really thick. The mixture should form stiff points when you lift the whisk up.

4 Gently fold in the sugar, a little bit at a time.

5 Place a sheet of greaseproof paper onto a baking tray, and spoon the mixture into a circle on it.

6 Ask your grown-up helper to put the tray in the oven and bake the meringue for forty-five minutes. When it's cooked, leave it to cool in the oven, then move it to a plate.

7 Pour the yogurt into the middle of the meringue and sprinkle the berries on top.

8 While the meringue is cooking, draw a picture of your ballerina, from the waist up, on your card. Cut it out and stick it to a lolly stick. Stick the lolly stick into the centre of the meringue, so that it looks like your ballerina's tutu.

Clown Cheesecake

Ingredients
- 1 cup strawberries, plus a couple of extra ones to decorate
- 12 digestive biscuits
- 500g/1lb 1oz mascarpone cheese
- 2 tablespoons butter or margarine
- 50g/2oz of icing sugar
- 2 red grapes

1 Put the digestive biscuits in a plastic bowl and use the end of a rolling pin to crush them into crumbs.

2 Ask your grown-up helper to melt the butter in a saucepan, and add the biscuit crumbs. Stir with a wooden spoon and make sure all the crumbs are coated with butter.

3 Put the crumbs into a greased, loose-bottomed cake tin and press flat with a wooden spoon.

4 Squash the cupful of strawberries with a fork, until they are all mushy. Add the icing sugar and the cheese, and mix well. Cover the biscuit base with the strawberry mixture.

5 Put it in the fridge to set for one to two hours.

6 When it is ready to serve, add a large strawberry for a nose, grapes for eyes, and a few slices of strawberry to make a smiley mouth for your clown.

Pumpkin Pie

Ingredients – makes one pie

- ready-made pastry case
- ¼ pumpkin, chopped into 2cm squares
- 1 tablespoon treacle
- 50g/2oz soft brown sugar
- 142ml/5fl oz double cream
- 2 eggs

1. Ask your grown-up helper to preheat the oven to 180C/360F/gas mark 4 and place a baking tray inside it to warm up.
2. Ask your grown-up helper to boil the pumpkin pieces in a saucepan for about five minutes, until soft.
3. Drain the water and put the pumpkin in a bowl. Use a potato masher to mash it up.
4. Crack two eggs into a second bowl and whisk them until frothy.
5. Ask your grown-up helper to heat the treacle, sugar and cream in a pan. Stir and simmer for two minutes.
6. Pour the cream mixture into the eggs and whisk. Add the pumpkin and stir well.
7. Put the pastry case on the warmed baking tray and carefully pour in the mixture. Ask your grown-up helper to bake it in the oven for 35-45 minutes. Allow to cool before serving.
8. If you like, you can use a little extra cream to decorate your pumpkin pie.

Moon Rocks

Ingredients - makes about 12 rocks

- 300g/10½ oz plain flour
- 100g/3½ oz butter or margarine
- ½ cup of raisins
- 100g/3½ oz sugar
- 1 egg, beaten
- blue food colouring (optional)
- marzipan and sweets to decorate (optional)

1 Ask your grown-up helper to preheat the oven to 200C/400F/gas mark 6.

2 Lightly grease a baking tray.

3 Using your fingers, rub the butter into the flour until the mixture looks like fine crumbs.

4 Add the sugar and raisins and mix.

5 Add the egg and a couple of drops of food colouring, if you are using it.

6 Mix everything together with your hands and form the dough into small balls.

7 Place them on the baking tray and bake for 15 minutes.

8 Whilst the moon rocks are cooking, make spaceship shapes with the marzipan.

9 Leave the cakes to cool before serving, then use the spaceships and raisins to decorate the plate.

Queen of Hearts Tarts

Ingredients - makes about 12 tarts
- packet shortcrust pasty
- jar of strawberry jam
- a little water
- some flour

You will also need:
- a circle-shaped cutter
- a heart-shaped cutter

1 Ask your grown-up helper to preheat the oven to 200C/400F/ gas mark 6.

2 Lightly grease a baking tray.

3 Sprinkle some flour on to a clean work surface and roll out the pastry.

4 Use the circle-shaped cutter to cut out as many circles as you can.

5 Use the heart-shaped cutter to cut hearts out of the middle of half of the circles.

6 Place the full circles on the greased baking tray and brush the edges of each one with a little water.

7 Place the circles with the hearts cut out over the top.

8 Put a teaspoon of jam in each heart. The jam will spread while cooking, so be careful not to put too much in.

9 Ask your grown-up helper to bake them in the oven for 15-20 minutes, until the pastry is golden.

10 Leave the tarts to cool before serving.

Seven Dwarfs Custard Pie

Ingredients - makes one pie
- packet shortcrust pastry
- 1 apple, sliced
- 1 carton ready-made custard
- 1 egg
- 3 tablespoons milk
- a little flour

You will also need:
- a gingerbread man cutter or the template opposite

1 Ask your grown-up helper to preheat the oven to 180C/350F/gas mark 4.

2 Lightly grease a baking tray.

3 Sprinkle some flour onto a clean work surface and roll out the pastry.

4 Place a saucer on the pastry and cut round it twice, so you have two circles of pastry.

5 Place one of the circles on the greased baking tray and cover it with the slices of apple. Leave a gap around the edge.

6 Break the egg into a cup and use a fork to beat it with the milk. Brush this mixture around the edges of the pastry circle.

7 Use the gingerbread man cutter or the template below to cut a man shape out of the middle of the second circle.

8 Place this circle on top of the first circle, pressing down the edges with a fork to make the pastry stick together.

9 Brush the top of the whole pie with the egg mixture.

10 Use a tablespoon to fill the man-shaped hole with custard.

11 Ask your grown-up helper to bake the pie in the oven for 30 minutes, until golden.

Choo-Choo Train

Ingredients - makes one train

- large chocolate Swiss roll
- 2 mini chocolate Swiss rolls
- 6 mini doughnuts
- jelly sweets
- 50g/2oz butter or margarine
- 100g/3½oz sugar
- 2 tablespoons cocoa powder
- 2 tablespoons water

1 Ask your grown-up helper to cut the larger Swiss roll in half.

2 Lay one piece on a large plate and put the other half upright at the end of it.

3 Mix the butter and sugar in a bowl until creamy, then add the cocoa powder and water, and mix again.

4 Stand one of the mini Swiss rolls upright on the end of the train as a chimney. Use a little of the icing to hold it in place.

5 Cut the second mini Swiss roll in half, and place half behind the chimney. Use the icing to stick this in place, too.

6 Use a spatula to spread the remaining icing all over the cake.

7 While the icing is still sticky, press three of the mini doughnuts onto each side, to make the wheels of the train.

8 Squash the jelly sweets into the centre of the doughnut wheels and around the cab to decorate it.

9 Put your Choo-Choo train in the fridge until the icing has set.

Gingerbread Robot

Ingredients - makes one robot
- 225g/8oz self-raising flour
- 100g/3½oz soft brown sugar
- 75g/2½oz butter or margarine
- 1 teaspoon ginger powder
- 2 tablespoons golden syrup
- 1 egg
- a little flour
- ready-made, rolled icing in various colours
- icing pens in various colours

1 Ask your grown-up helper to preheat the oven to 170C/325F/gas mark 3.

2 Lightly grease a baking tray.

3 Put the flour, ginger and sugar into a large bowl. Add the butter or margarine and rub it into the mixture with your fingers, until it looks like fine breadcrumbs.

4 Break the egg into a cup and beat it with a fork. Add the golden syrup and mix.

5 Add the egg mixture to the breadcrumbs and stir with a spoon. As it thickens, mix it with clean hands instead. It might be a bit crumbly at first, but keep kneading until it forms a stiff dough.

6 Sprinkle some flour onto a clean work surface and keep kneading the dough until it is completely mixed.

7 Roll the dough out very thinly.

8 Ask your grown-up helper to cut out two small circles for hands, a small square for a head, a larger square for the body, and four rectangles for the arms and legs.

9 Use a fish slice to place all the pieces on the greased baking tray, making the shape of your robot.

10 Ask your grown-up helper to bake it in the oven for 15-20 minutes.

11 Leave the gingerbread robot to cool on a wire rack.

12 Roll the icing out thinly and cut shapes to decorate your robot. You can also use the icing pens or sweets.

Jazzy Microphone

Ingredients
- 2 oranges
- 284ml double cream
- 3 tablespoons runny honey
- 1 tablespoon cornflour
- ½ cup water
- ice cream cones
- liquorice Catherine wheel
- icing pen
- jelly sweets

To make the ice cream

1 Finely grate the rind of the oranges into a bowl.

2 Peel the remaining skin from the oranges and chop them into small pieces.

3 Ask your grown-up helper to put the orange pieces, grated rind, honey, cornflour and water into a saucepan, and heat the mixture.

4 Keep stirring the mixture until it thickens, then let it cool down completely.

5 Meanwhile, pour the cream into a large bowl and whisk it until stiff.

6 Fold the orange mixture into the cream with a metal spoon. Pour it into a freezer-container and ask your grown-up helper to pop it in the freezer overnight.

To decorate the microphone

1 Unwind the liquorice Catherine wheel and cut a piece to fit around the top of the cone. Use the icing to stick the liquorice around the rim of the cone.

2 Spread some more icing on the cone and wind the liquorice round the handle to cover it.

3 Use the icing pen to stick the jelly sweets on, to make your ice cream cone look like a microphone!

4 When the microphone cones are ready, put a scoop of ice cream in the top of each one to serve.

Disco Pops

Ingredients - for 8 lollies

- 1 ½ litres lemonade
- jelly sweets (you could use fruit pieces as a healthier alternative)

You will also need:

- 8 plastic cups
- lolly sticks
- sticky tape
- scissors

1 Put about ten jelly sweets into each cup, and press them up against the sides.

2 Fill the cups up with lemonade.

3 Stick a strip of sticky tape across the top of each cup.

4 Ask your grown-up helper to snip a little slit in the sticky tape, in the middle of the cup.

5 Slide a lolly stick through the slit in the sticky tape. Don't push it down to the bottom of the cup. Make sure you leave enough sticking out to make a handle for your lollipop.

6 Ask your grown-up helper to stand them carefully in the freezer until they are frozen solid.

7 Remove the sticky tape and take the lollipops out of the cup moulds when you're ready to eat them.

Farmyard Smoothies

Ingredients
- 1 banana, sliced
- 1 cup milk
- 1 tablespoon yogurt

You will also need:
- card, round-ended scissors, sticky tape and colouring pens or pencils.

1 Peel the banana, break it into pieces and use a fork to mash it up in a bowl.

2 Add the yogurt, and stir.

3 Pour the milk into the mixture and whisk everything up.

4 Pour into a glass.

5 Draw a chick, cut it out and stick it to your glass to make a yellow chick drink.

Iceberg Slush

Ingredients
- a handful of strawberries or any other fruit, chopped up
- 1 cup orange juice
- 1 cup lemonade
- a jug of water
- a wedge of lemon
- 2 tablespoons sugar
- 2 ice cube trays

1 Pour the orange juice into an ice cube tray.

2 Put the chopped strawberries into another ice cube tray and fill it up with water. Ask your grown-up helper to put both trays in the freezer until the ice cubes have set.

3 Rub the lemon wedge around the rim of a glass. Pour the sugar onto a saucer, and dip the rim of the glass into the sugar, so that the sugar sticks to the lemon juice. Leave it to dry.

4 When they are frozen, put the orange ice cubes into a plastic jug and mash them into slush with the end of a rolling pin.

5 Spoon half of the mixture into a glass, then add a couple of the strawberry ice cubes. Fill up the glass with lemonade to serve.

Always ask your grown-up to help you with the freezer, because it's COLD COLD COLD!

Wake Up Juice

Ingredients - makes two large glasses

- 20 strawberries
- 500ml/17½fl oz apple juice, chilled
- 3 kiwis, peeled

You will also need:

- drinking straw
- card
- colouring pens or pencils
- safety scissors
- glue

1 Wash the strawberries and put them in a freezer bag. Ask your grown-up helper to put them in the freezer until frozen.

2 Fold a piece of card in half and draw Sleeping Beauty's head on one side. Carefully cut out the shape through both halves of the card, so that you have two heads. On one side, draw Sleeping Beauty with her eyes closed, on the other side, draw her with her eyes open. Glue the heads back to back, with the drinking straw in the middle.

3 Mash the kiwis in a bowl, then add half of the apple juice. Pour the mixture through a sieve, into a jug. Squash the pulp against the sieve with a wooded spoon, to get all the juice. Throw away the seeds and pulp that are left in the sieve. Put the jug of juice in the fridge until the strawberries are ready.

4 Put the frozen strawberries into a blender or food processor. Pour the remaining apple juice on top. Blend until the strawberries are crushed, but not too smooth.

5 Spoon the strawberry ice into a tall glass, then pour the kiwi juice over the top.

6 Stick your Sleeping Beauty straw into the drink so she looks like she is sleeping. Once you have drunk your drink, turn her around to wake up!

Big Cook's Word List

Baking tray a metal sheet used for cooking food in the oven.

Beat stir quickly with a fork, wooden spoon or electric whisk.

Dough a thick, stretchy mixture made from flour and liquid.

Freeze put food in the freezer until it is cold and hard.

Grate make food into small shreds by rubbing against a grater.

Grease rub with margarine or butter, so that food doesn't stick.

Knead mix together with your hands, to make dough.

Peel take the skin off a fruit or vegetable.

Preheat switch the oven on so it can heat up, before you need to use it.

Simmer keep the water bubbling gently, but not boiling.

Spatula flat, blunt tool used for mixing and spreading.

Tablespoon large spoon used for serving food. Approximately 15ml.

Teaspoon small spoon used for stirring tea. Approximately 5ml.